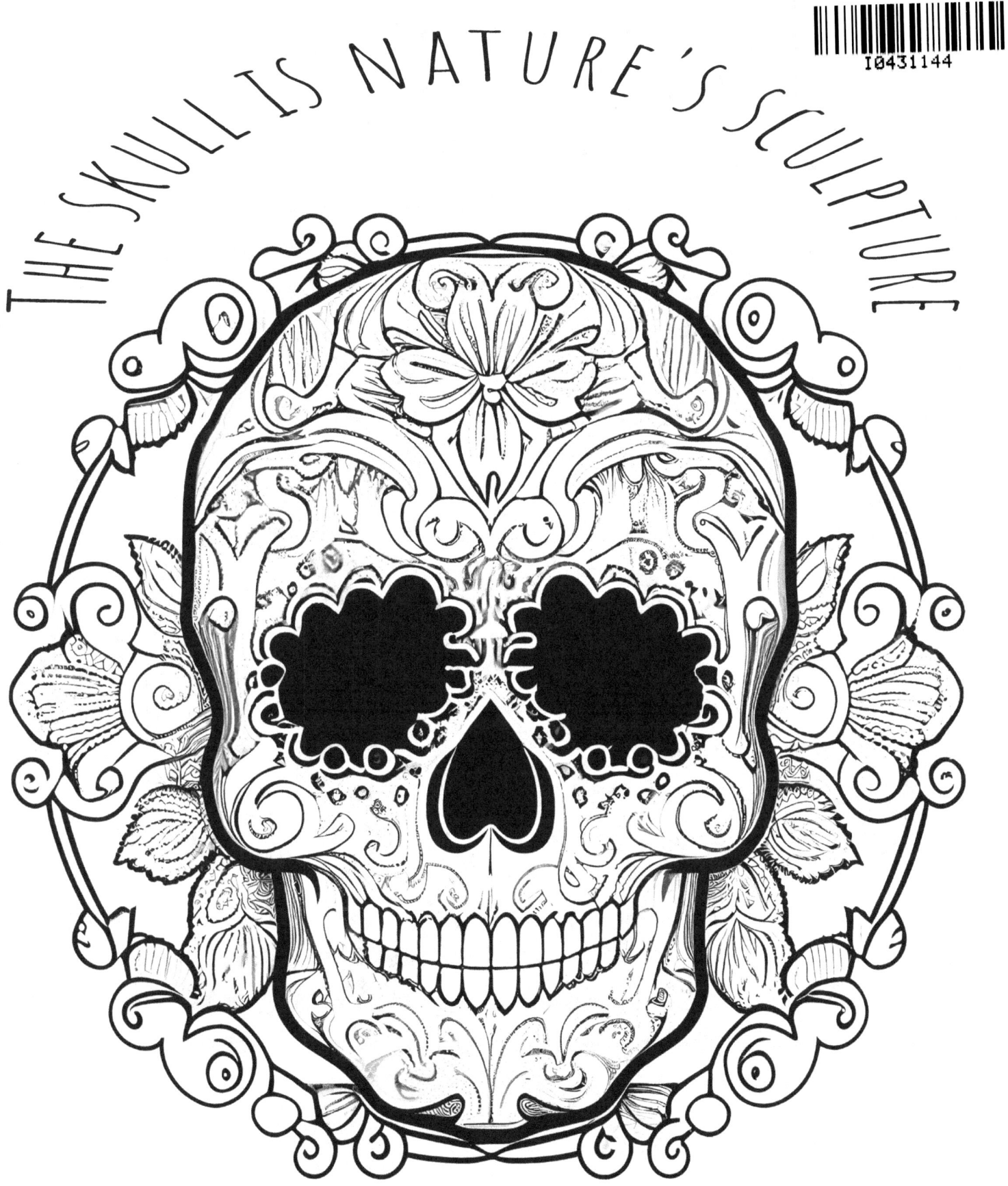

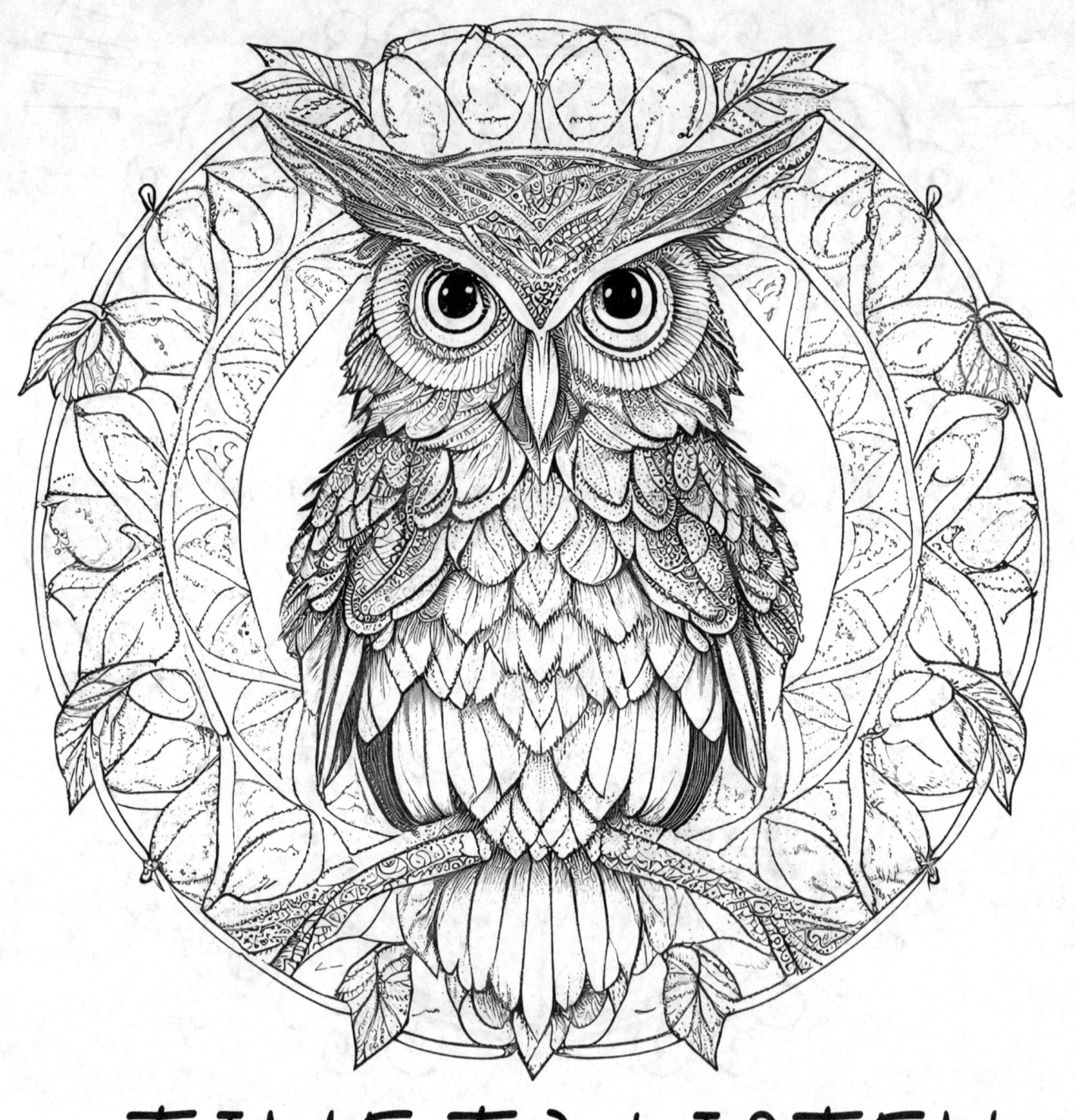

Flowers always make people better

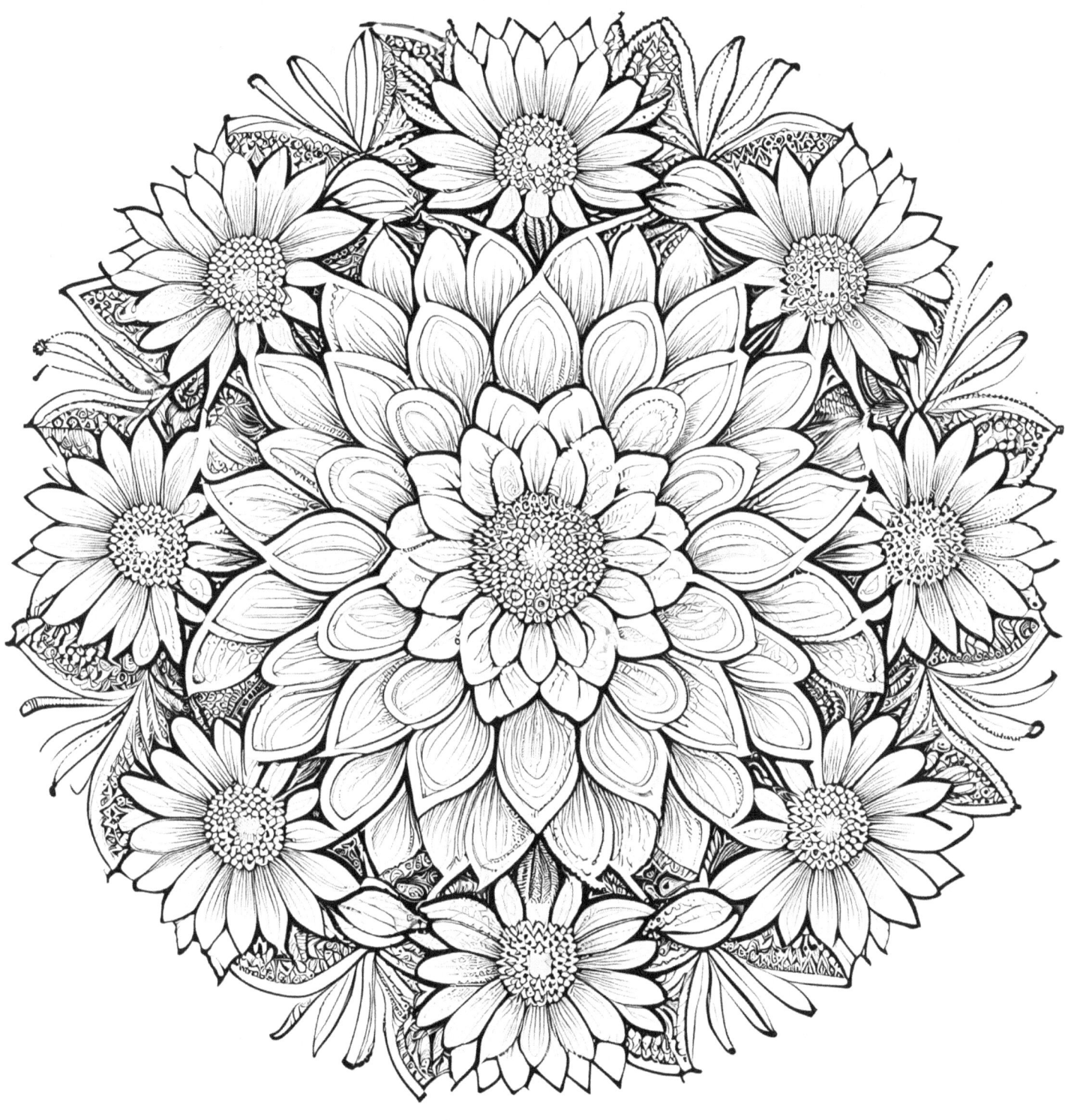

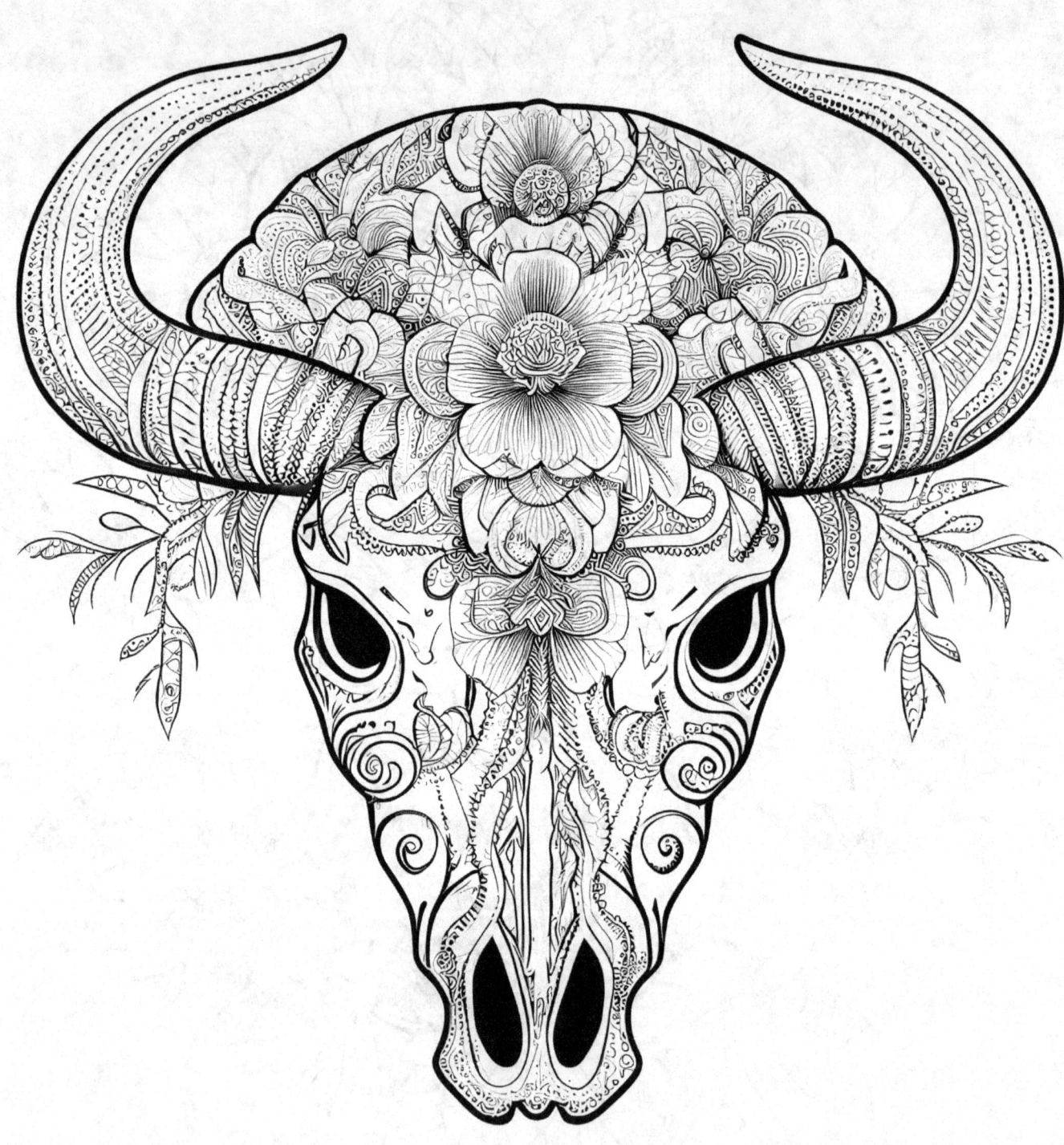

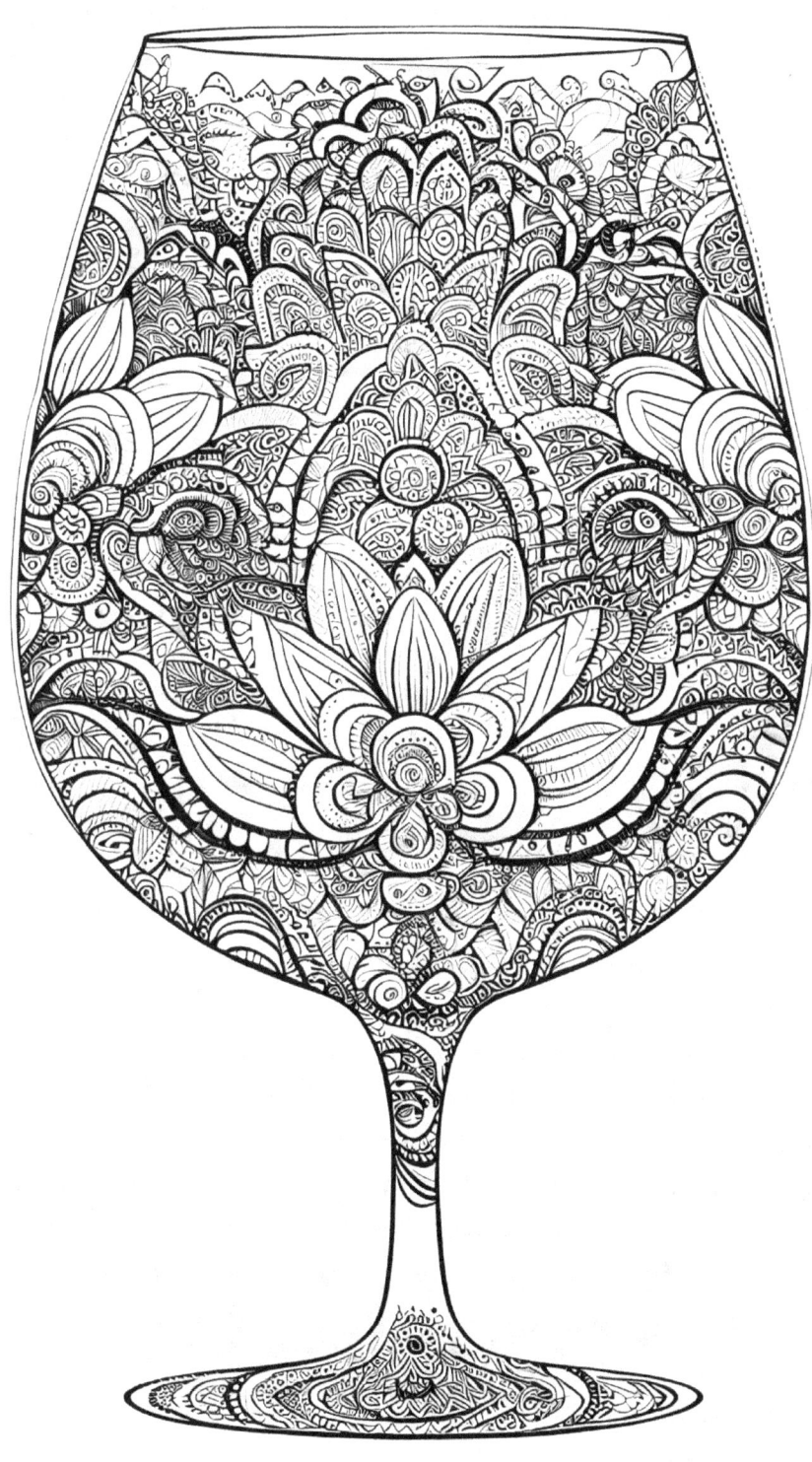

"Great Things Begin From Inside"

FREEDOM IS A STATE OF MIND

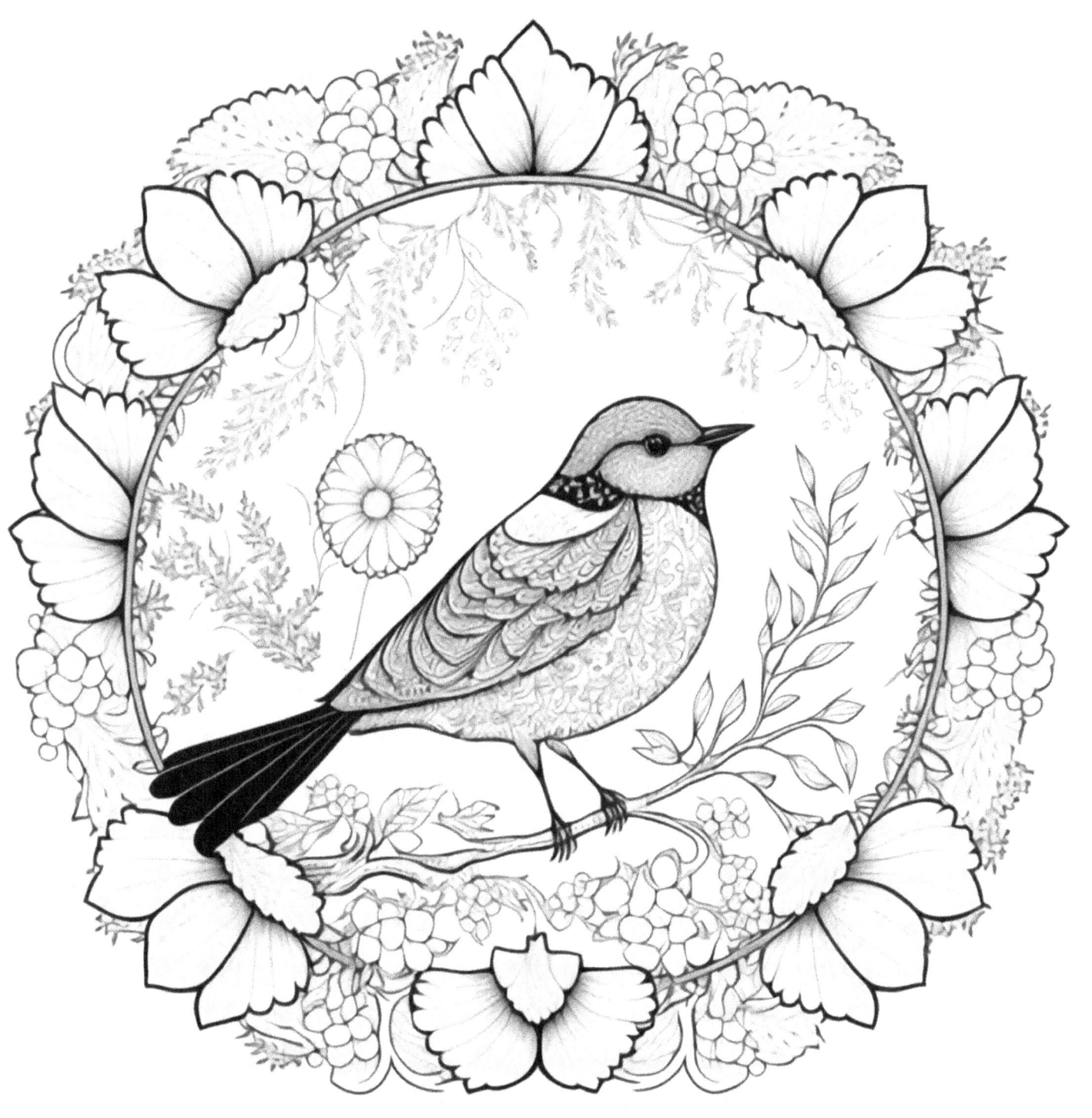

Let Your Dream Set Sail!

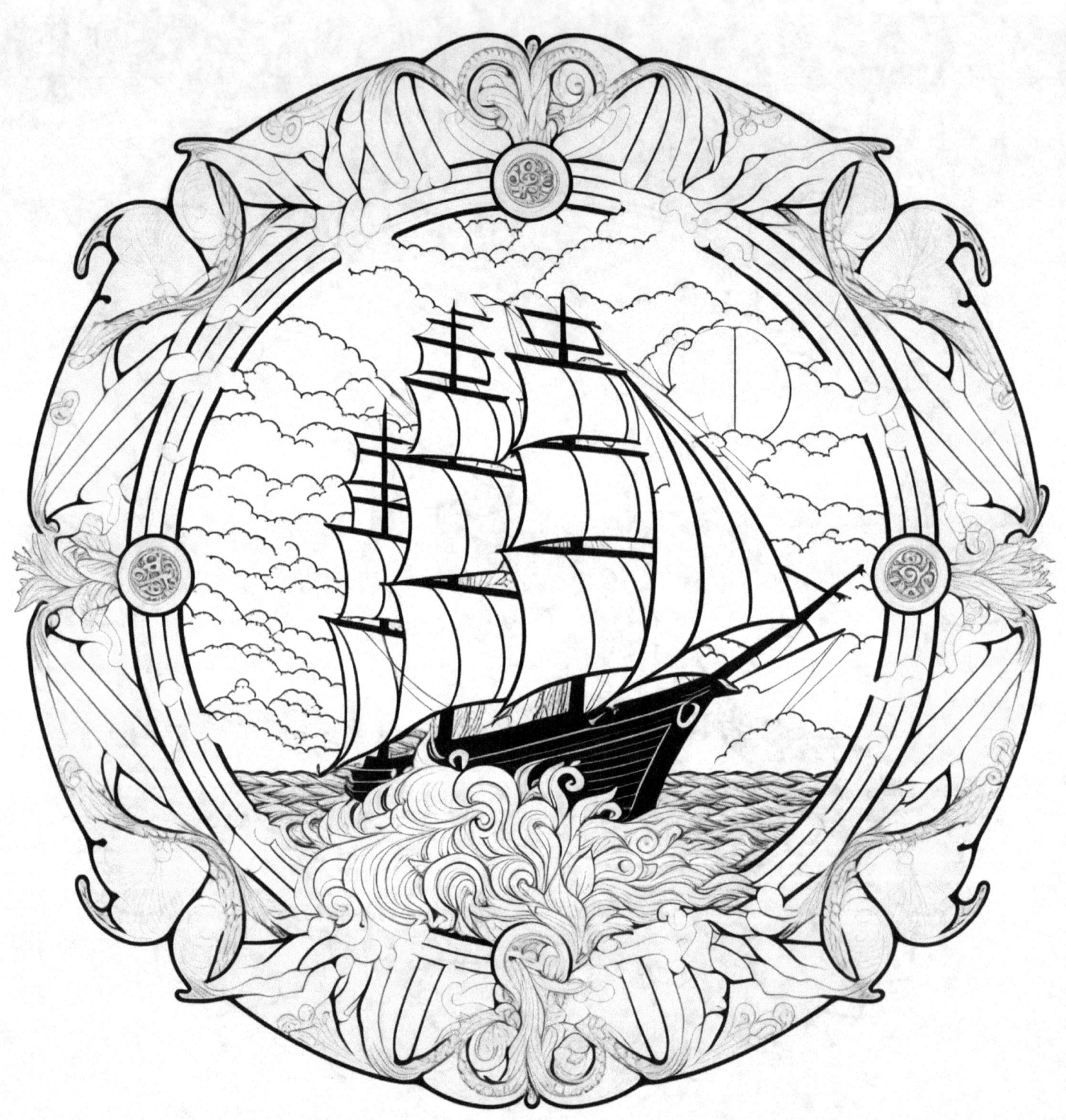

Stay Wild And Be Free

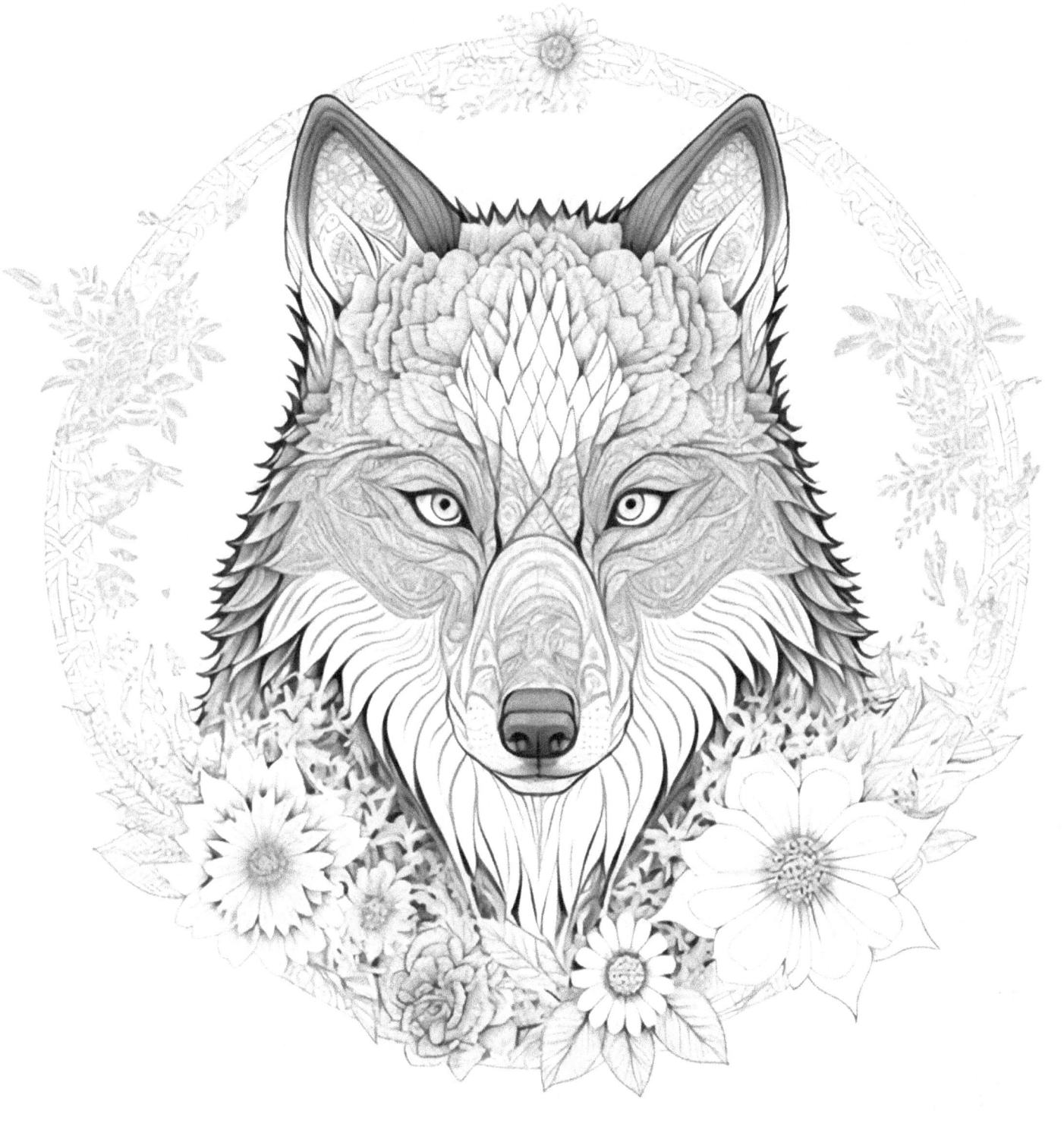

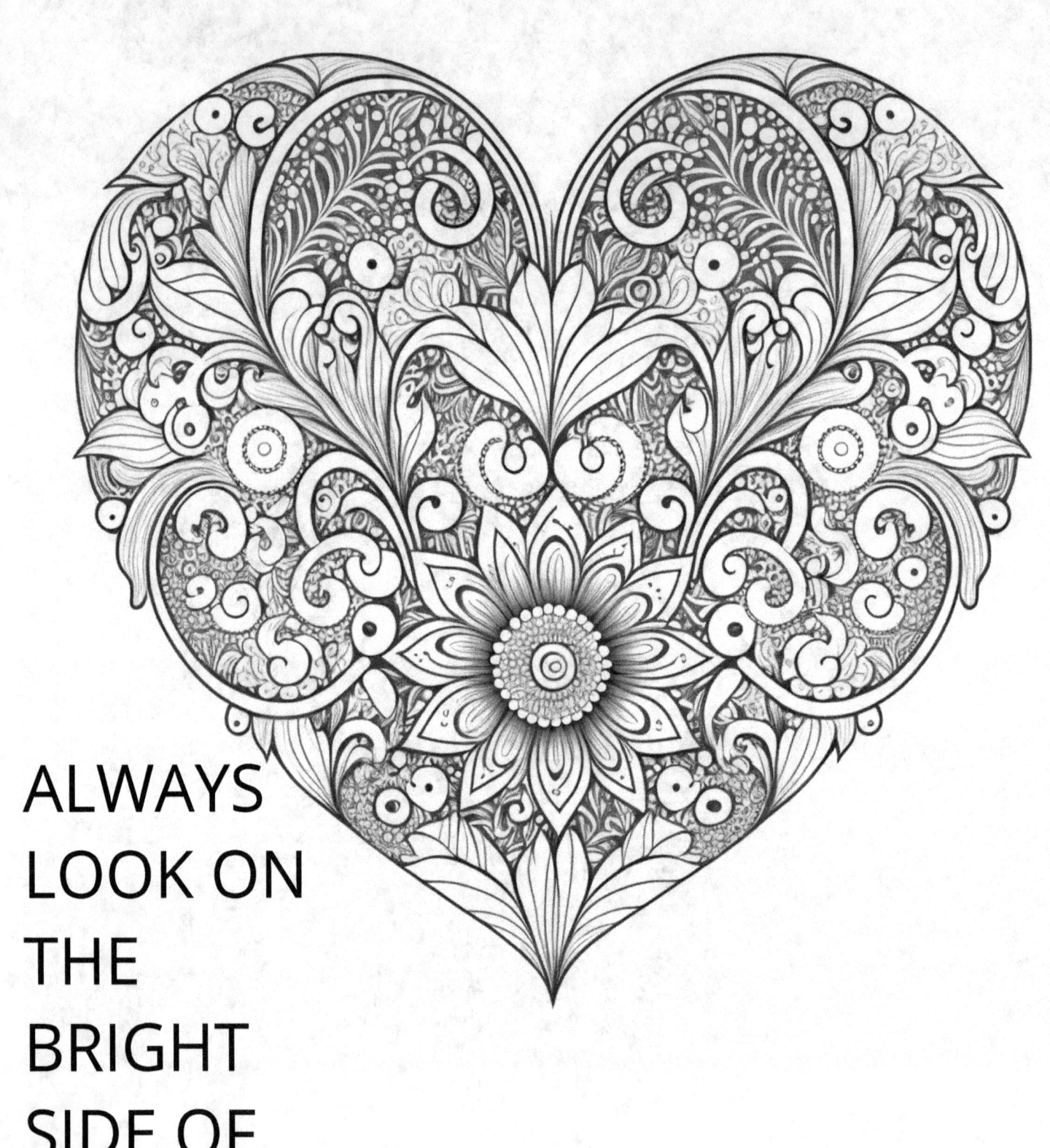

ALWAYS LOOK ON THE BRIGHT SIDE OF LIFE

YOUR LIFE IS CONTROLLED BY

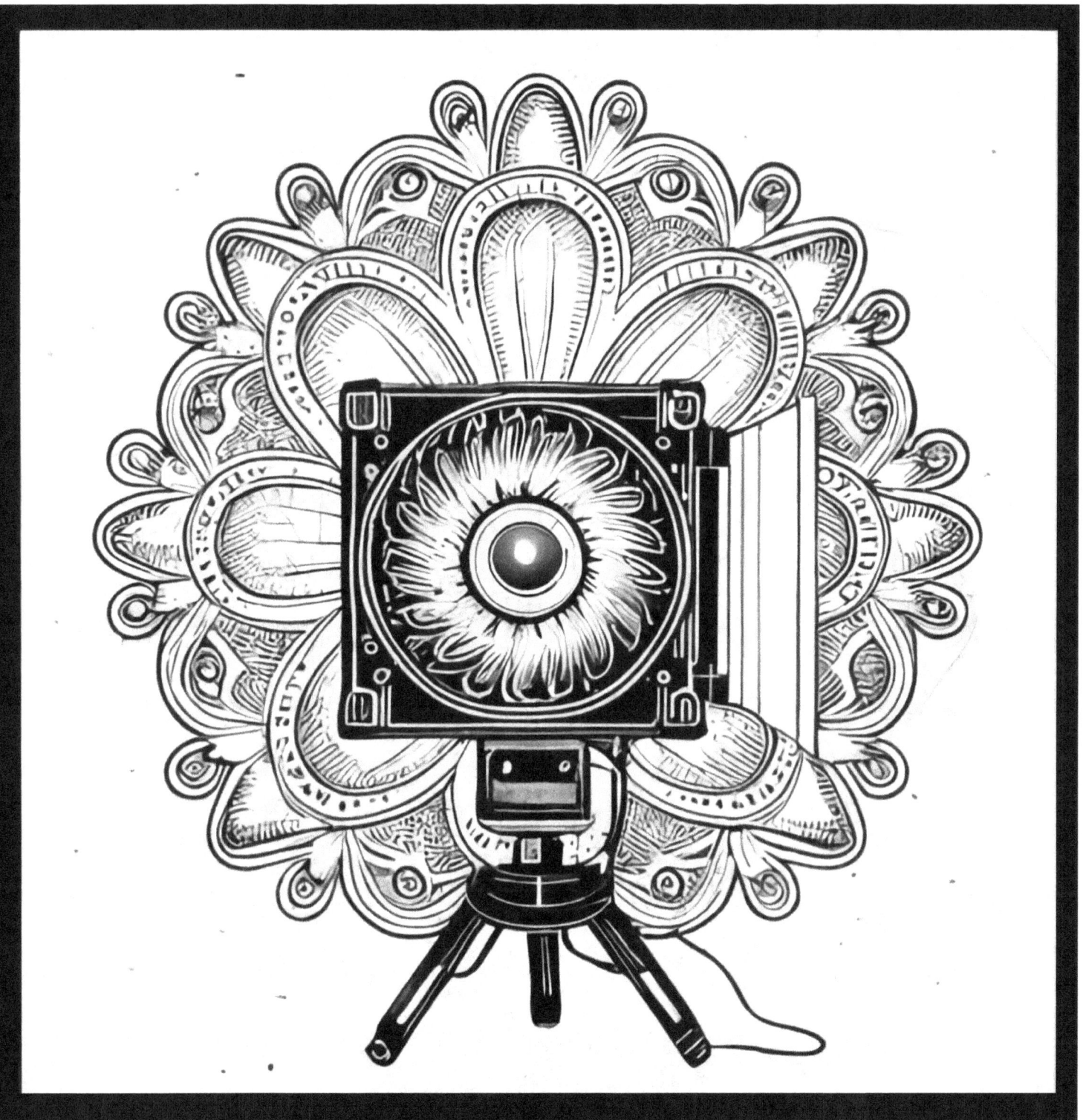

WHAT YOU FOCUS ON

MUSIC IS LIFE
THAT'S WHY OUR
HEARTS HAVE
BEAT

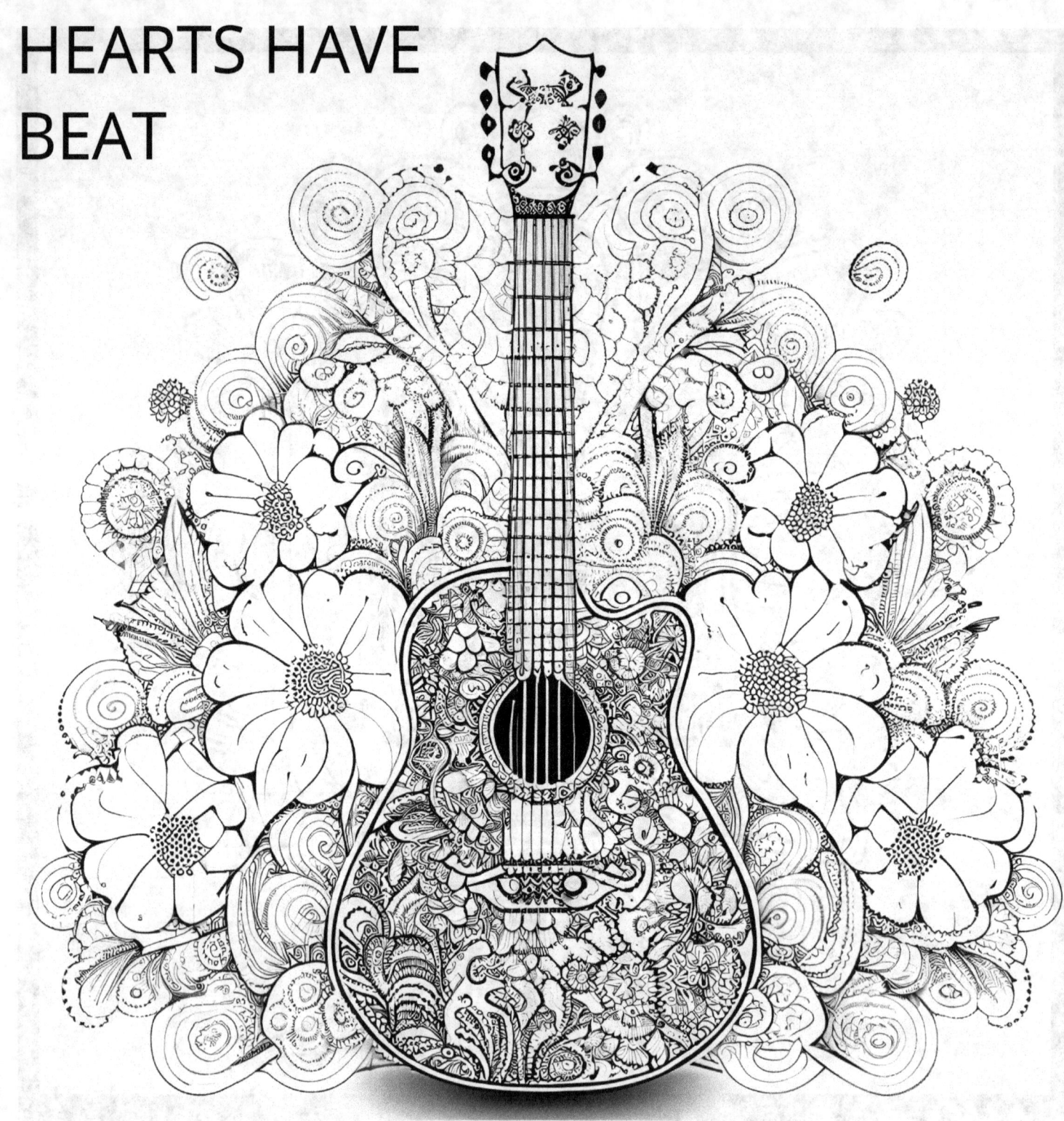

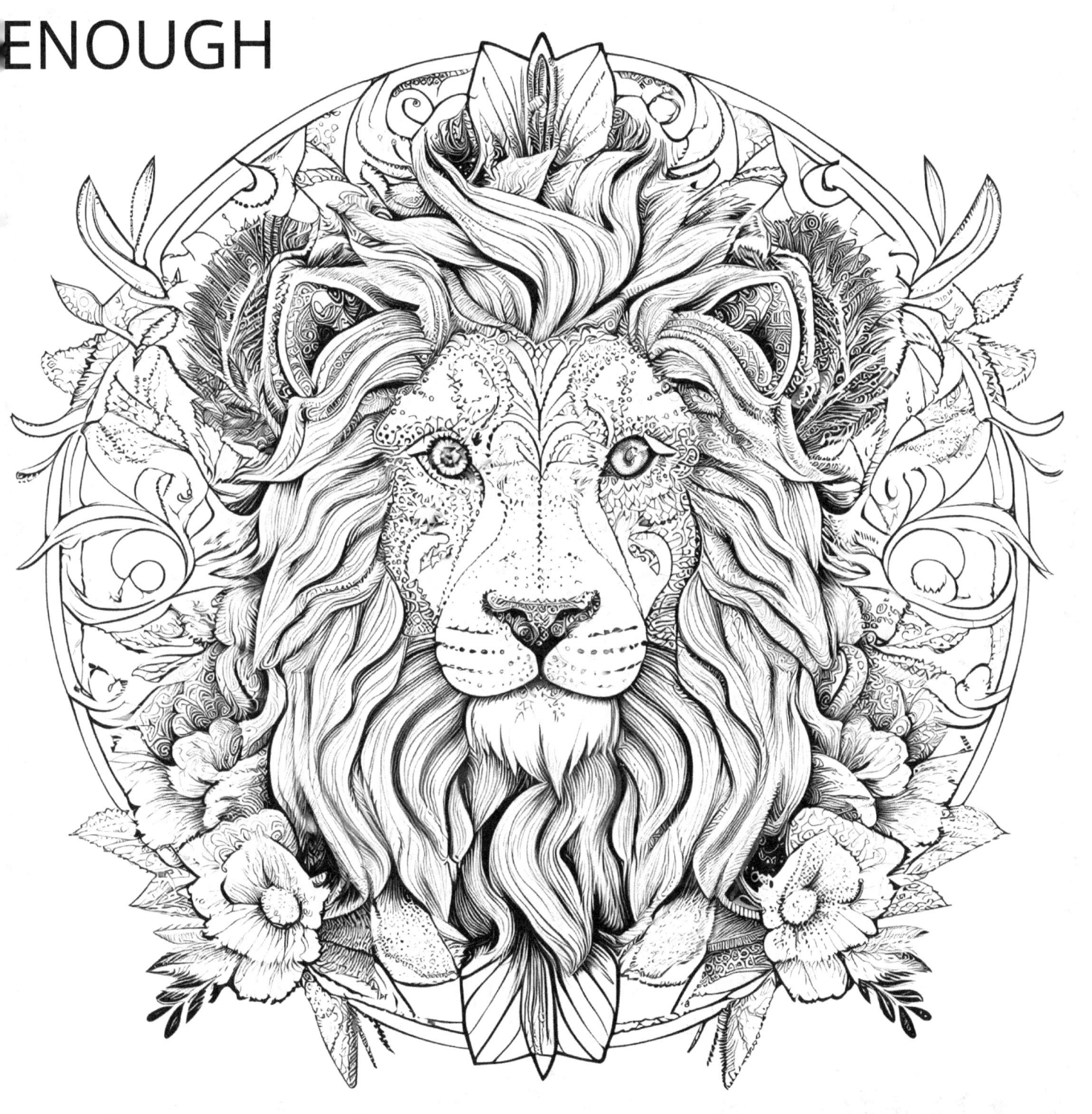

SETTING A GOAL IS NOT ENOUGH

HUNT THEM!

Life Begins At The End Of Your Comfort Zone

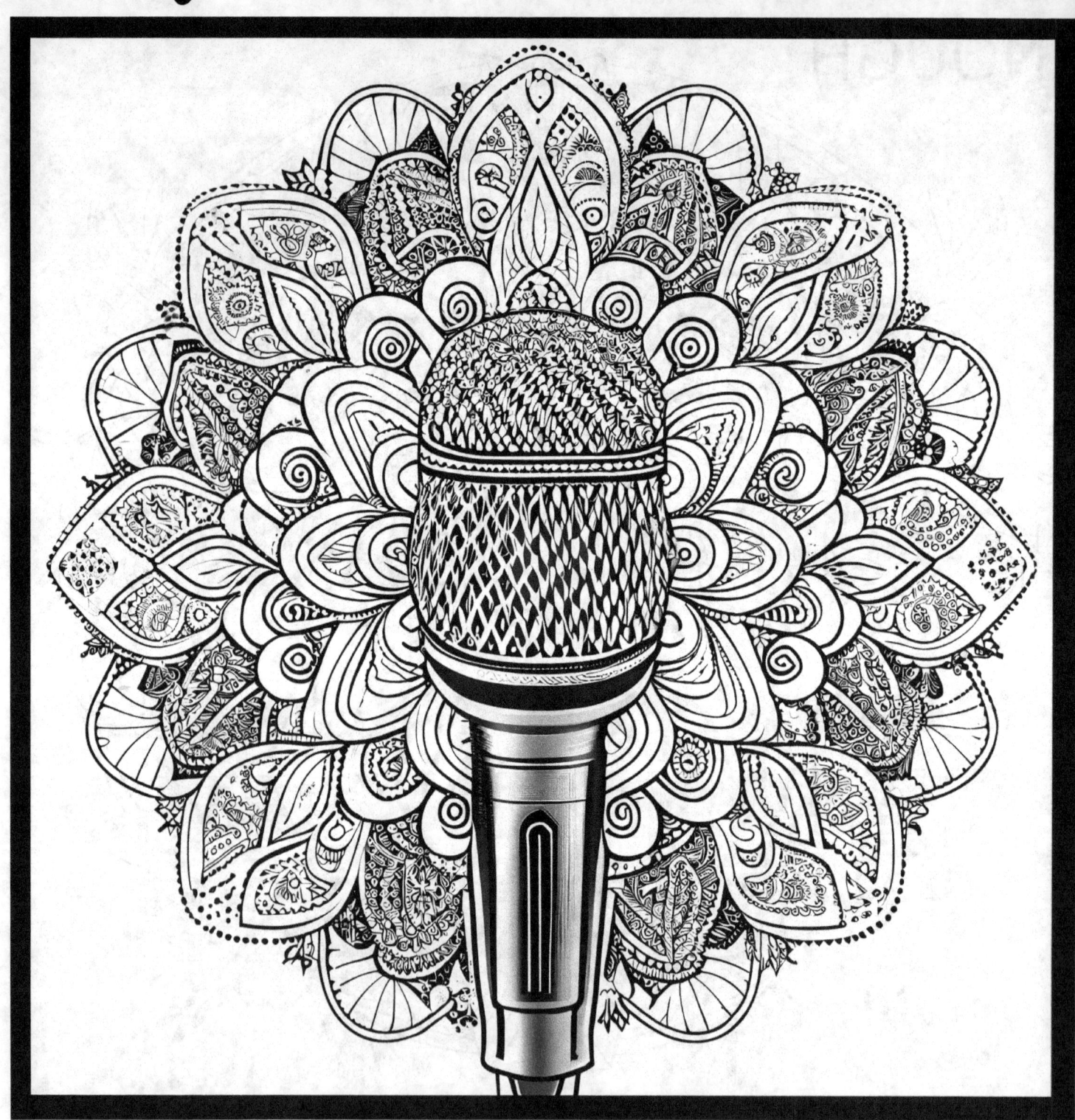

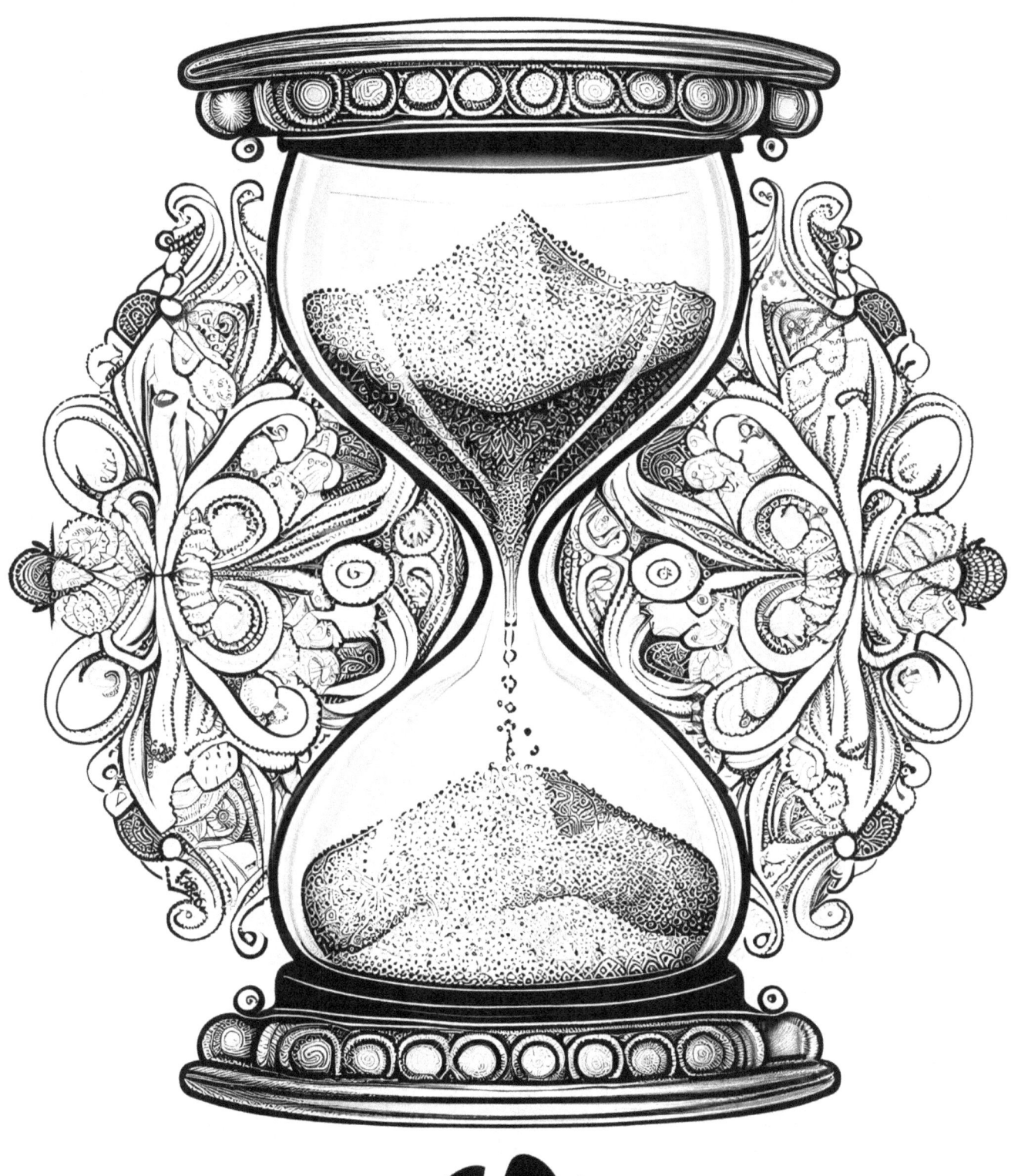

"THE SEA TURTLES STORES ITS WISDOM IN HIS SHELL" UNKNOWN

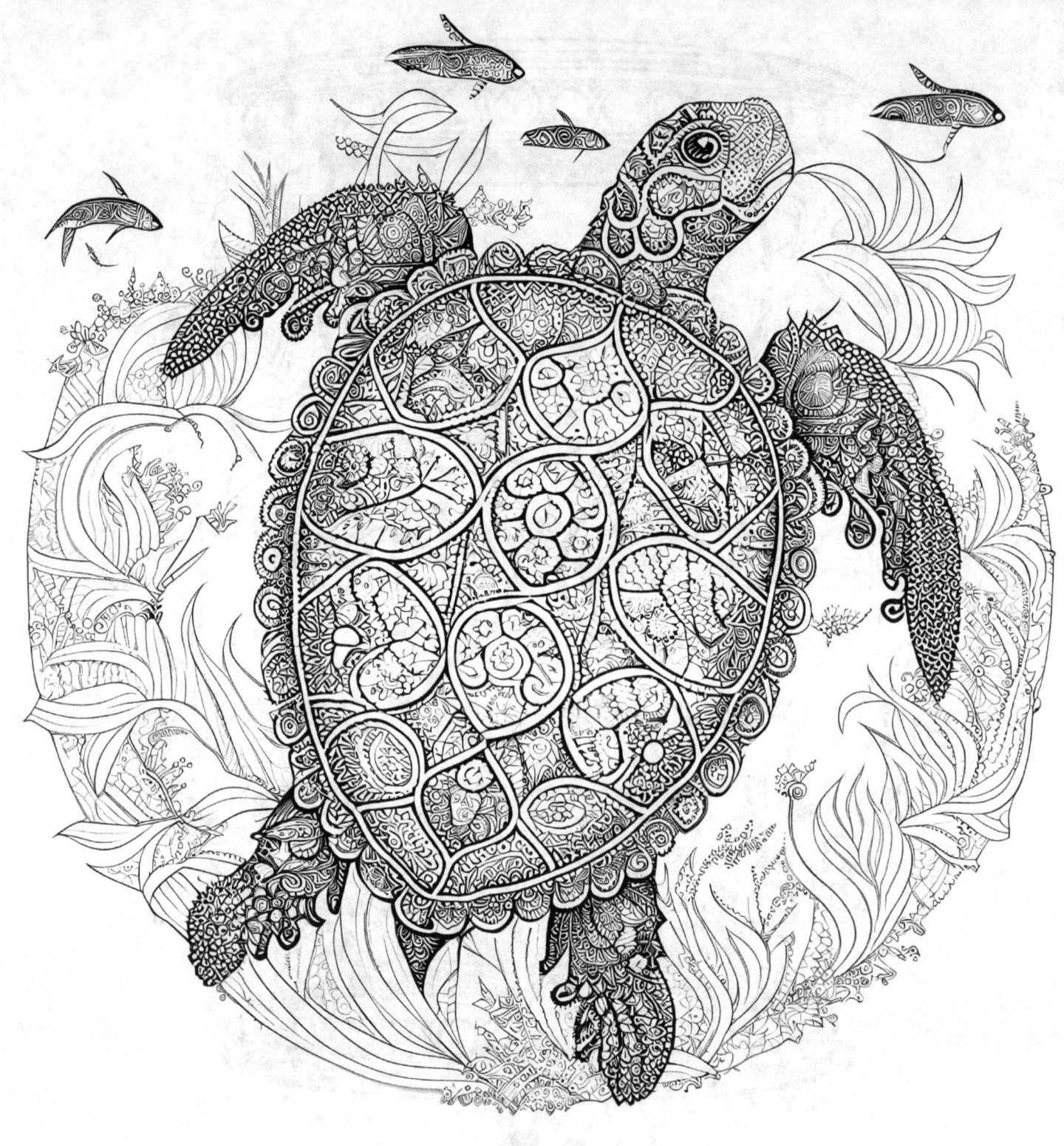

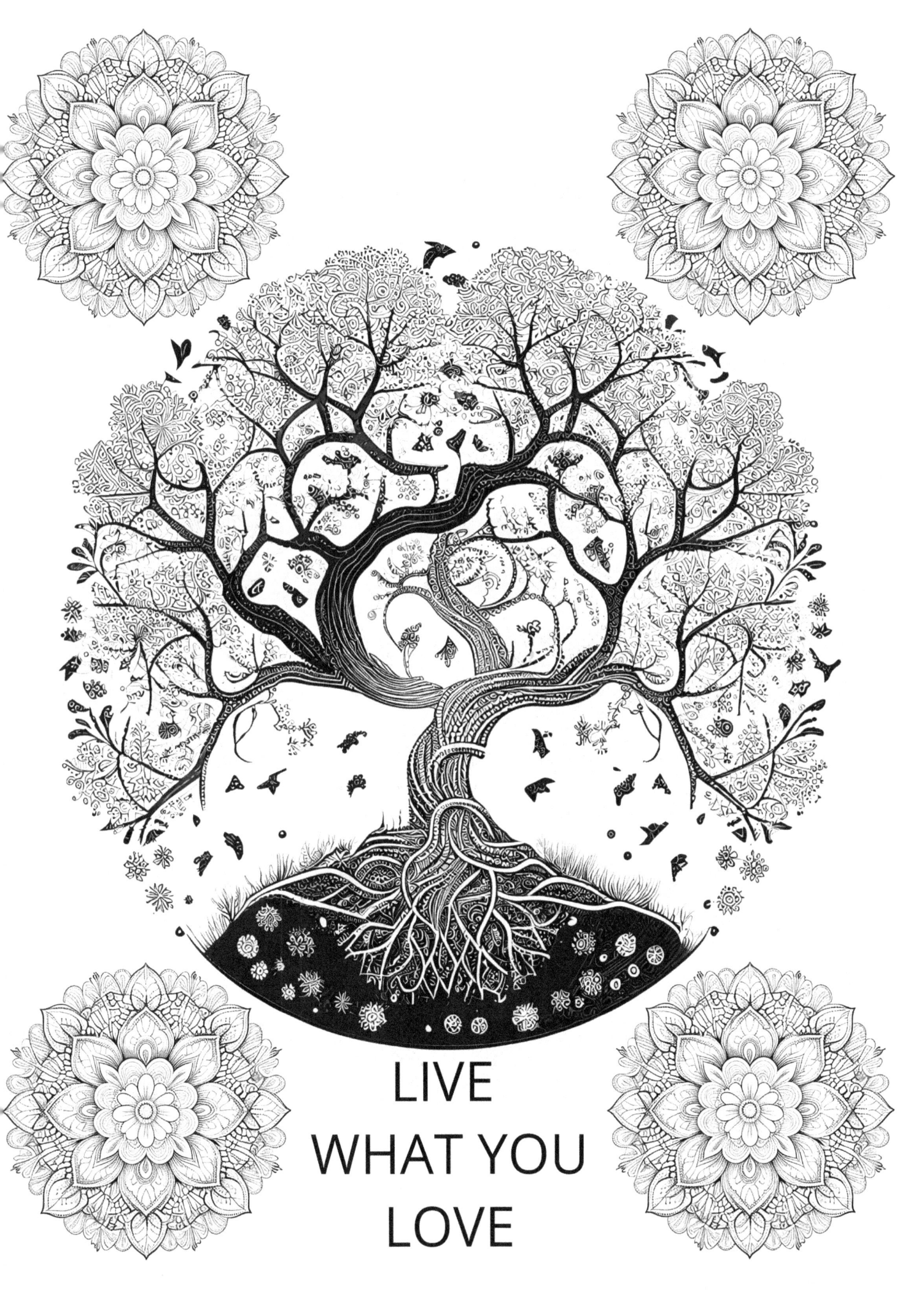

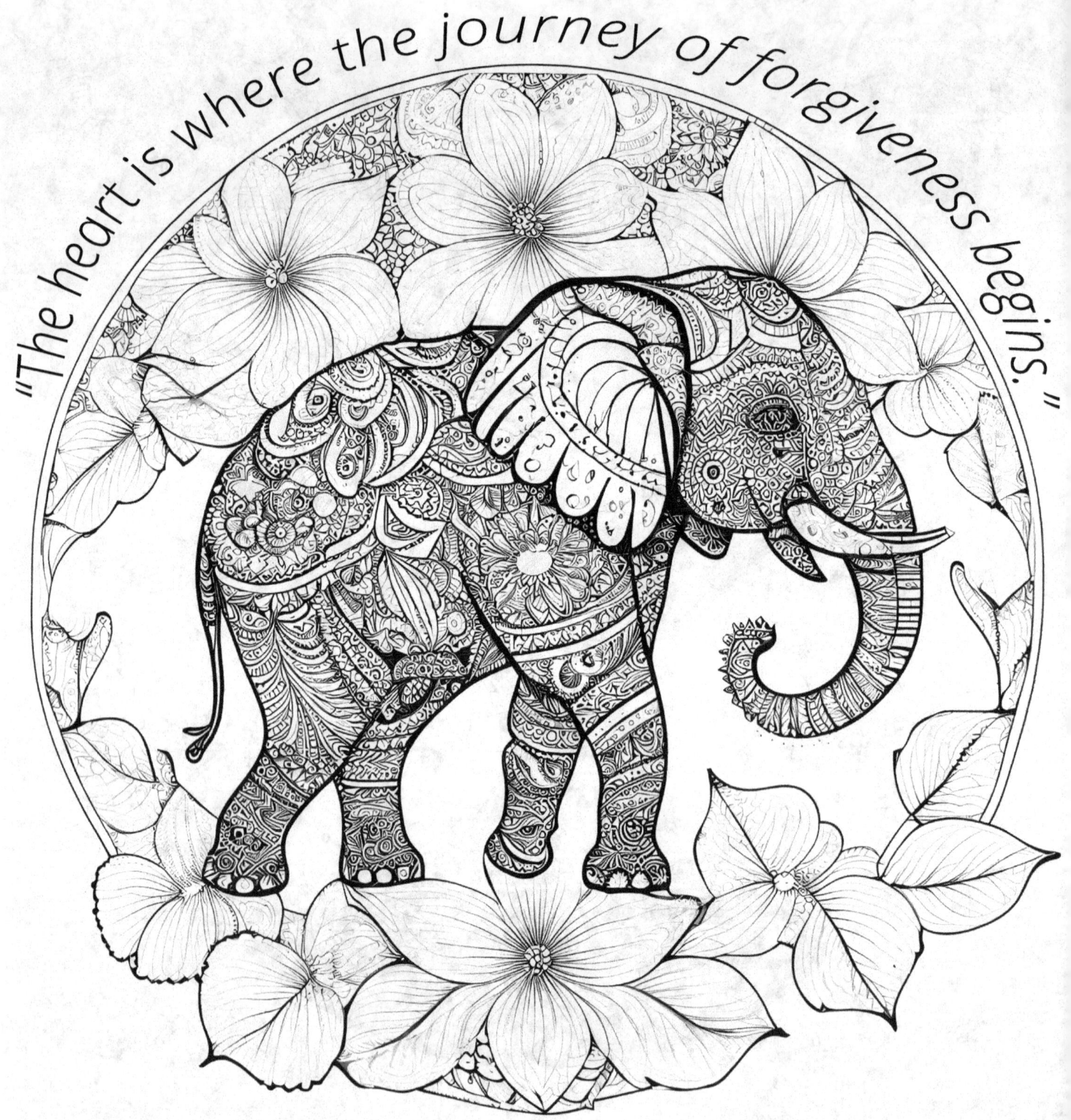
"The heart is where the journey of forgiveness begins."

IT IS ONLY IN THE MICROSCOPE THAT OUR LIFE LOOKS SO BIG

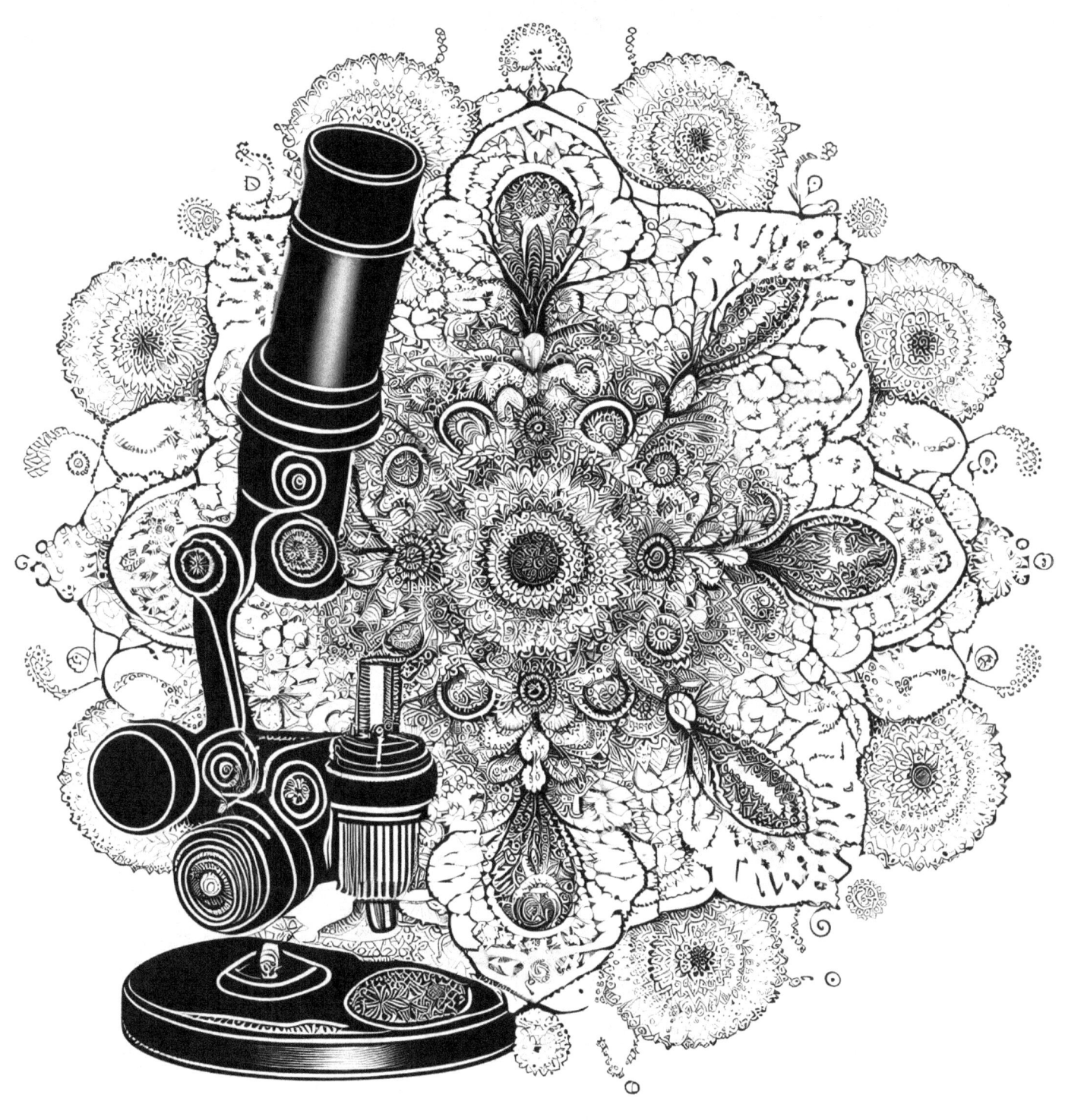

LIFE IS LIKE A CUP OF COFFEE OR TEA. NO MATTER HOW BITTER IT MAY BE, IT IS ALWAYS ENJOYABLE.

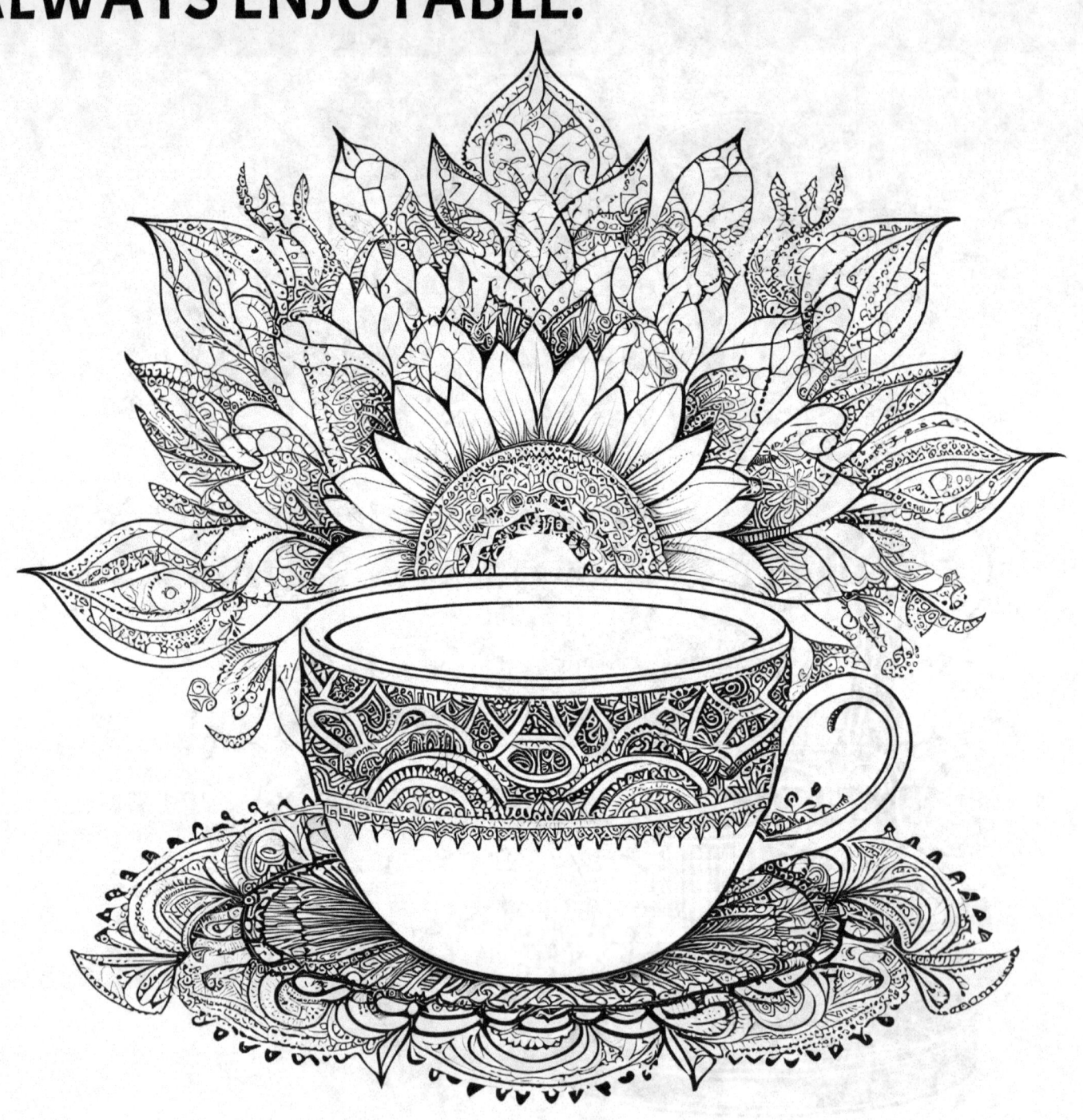

IF YOU STICK TO THE FAMILIAR YOU WON'T FIND THE

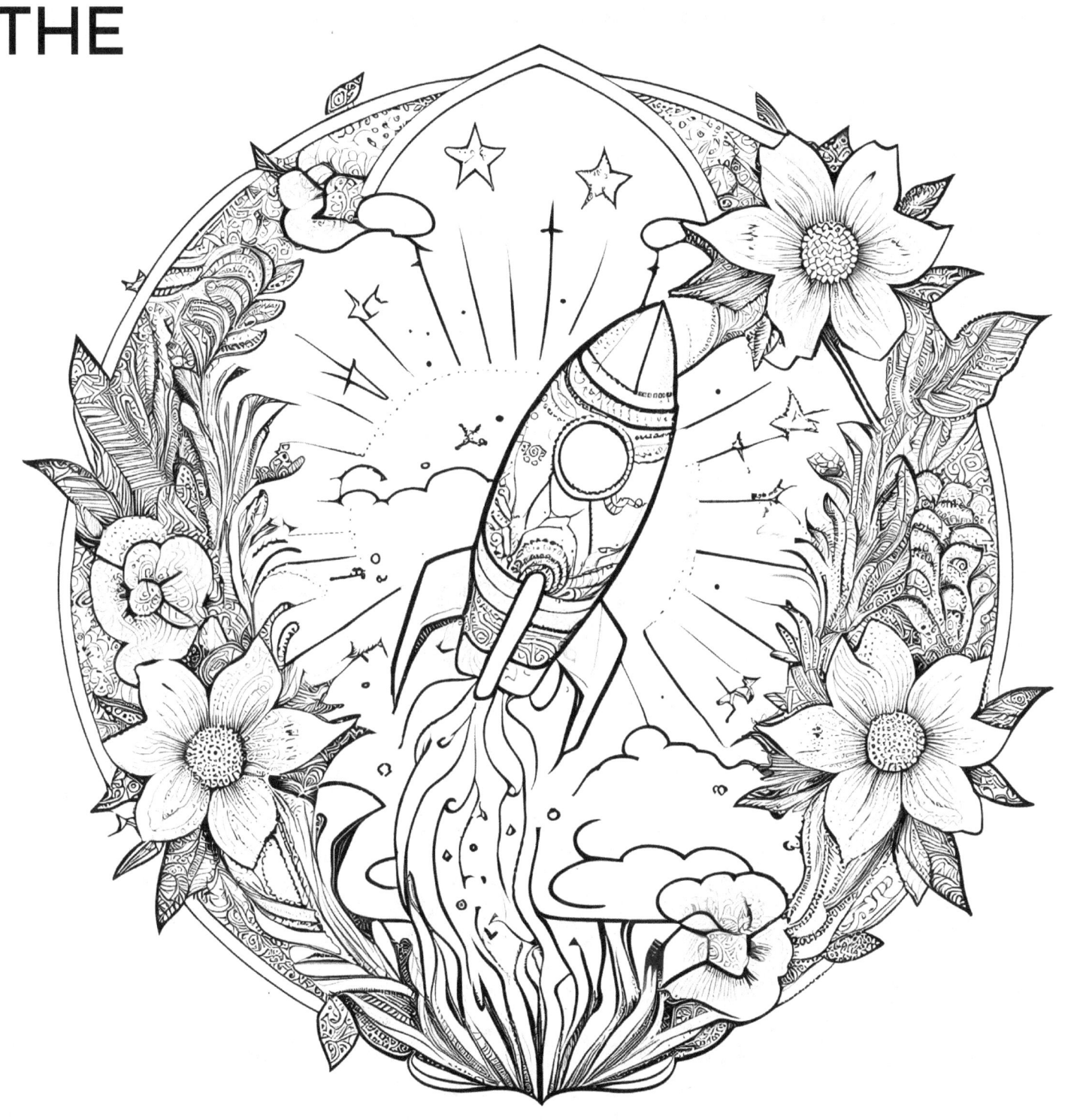

UNEXPECTED

A teapot can represent at the same time the comforts of solitude

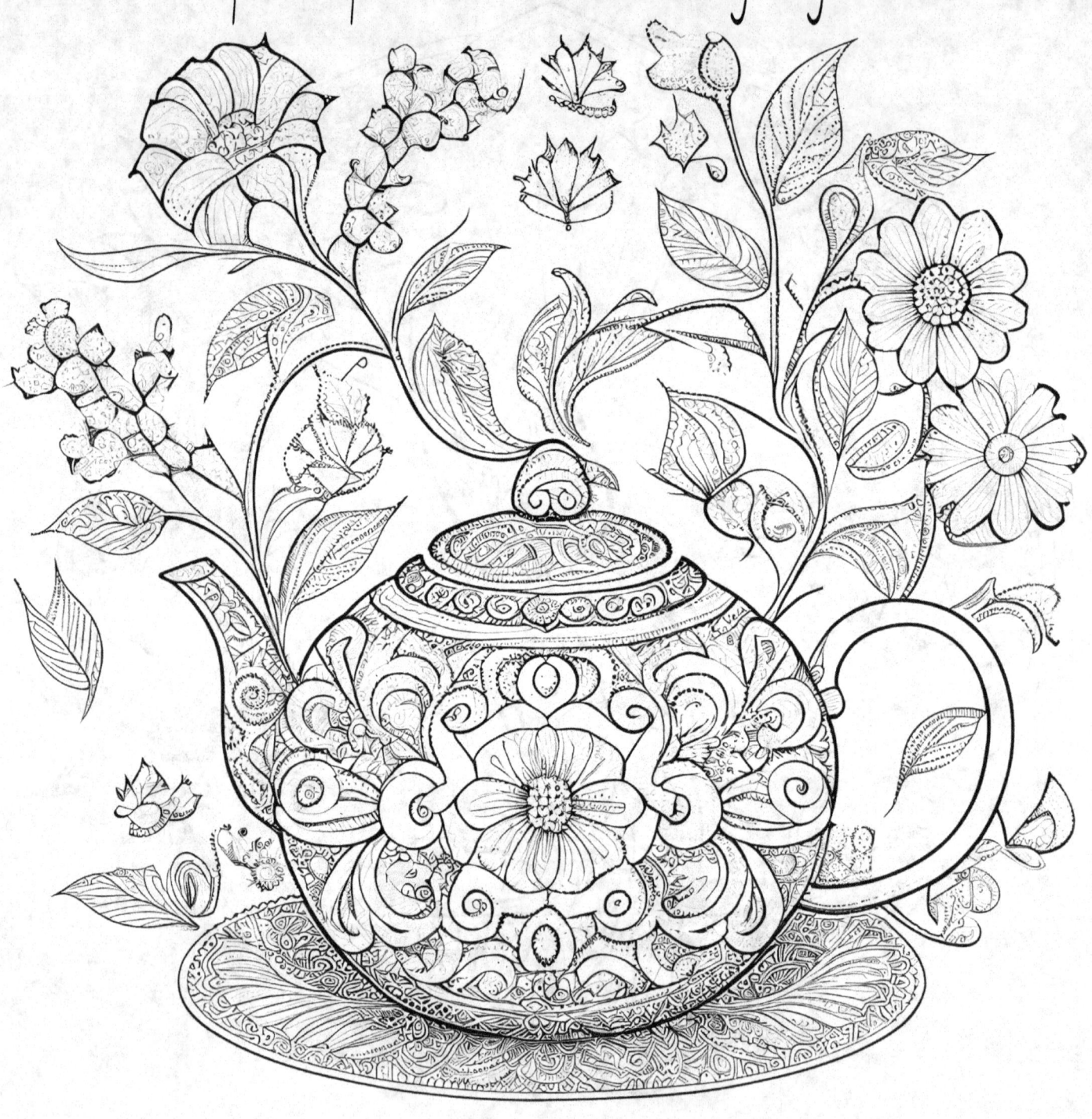

and the pleasures of company

A sword, a spade, and a thought should never be allowed to rust.

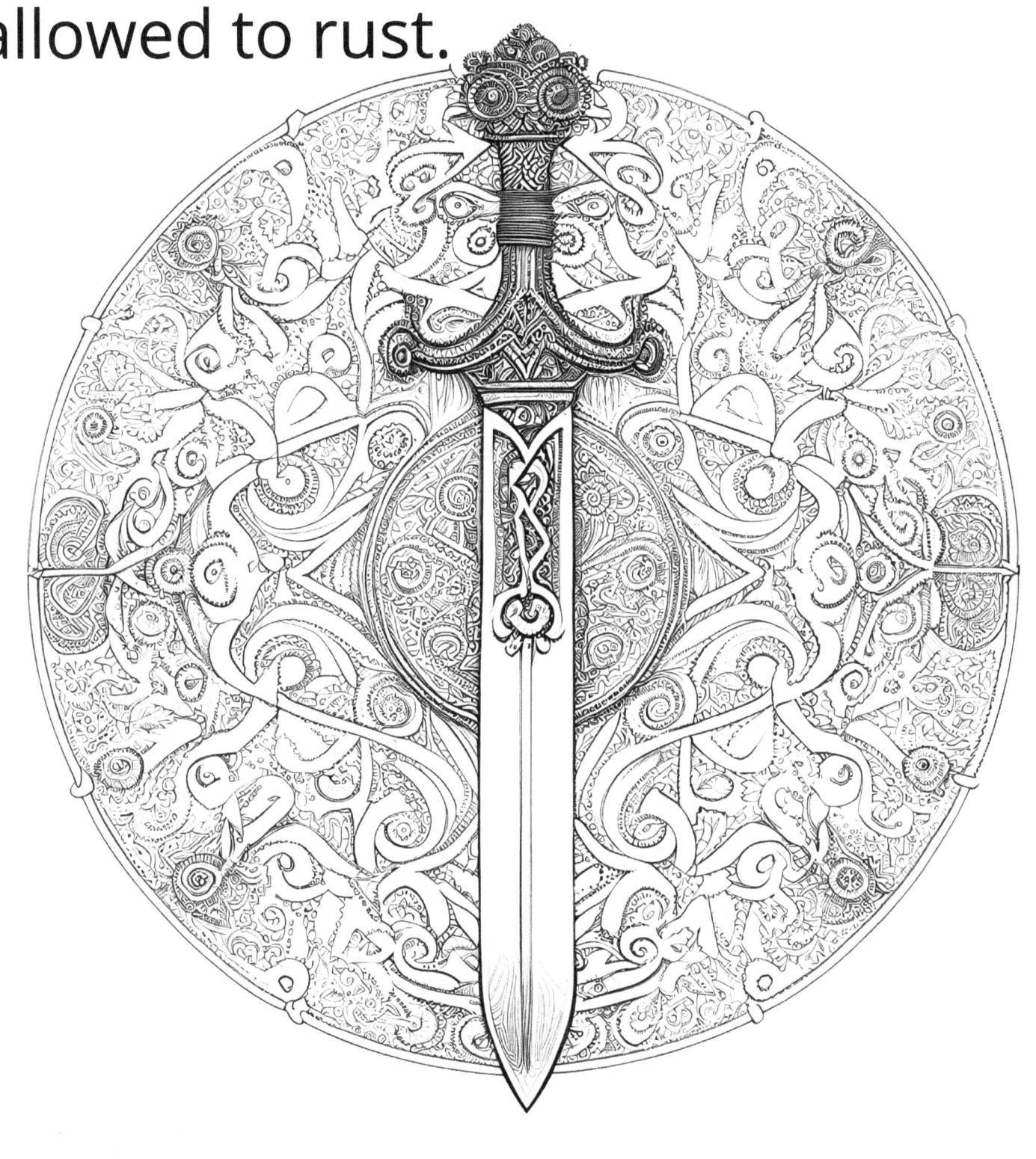

IN THE PAST, PEOPLE WERE BORN ROYAL. NOWADAYS, ROYALTY COMES FROM WHAT YOU DO.

BE THE REASON SOMEONE SMILES TODAY

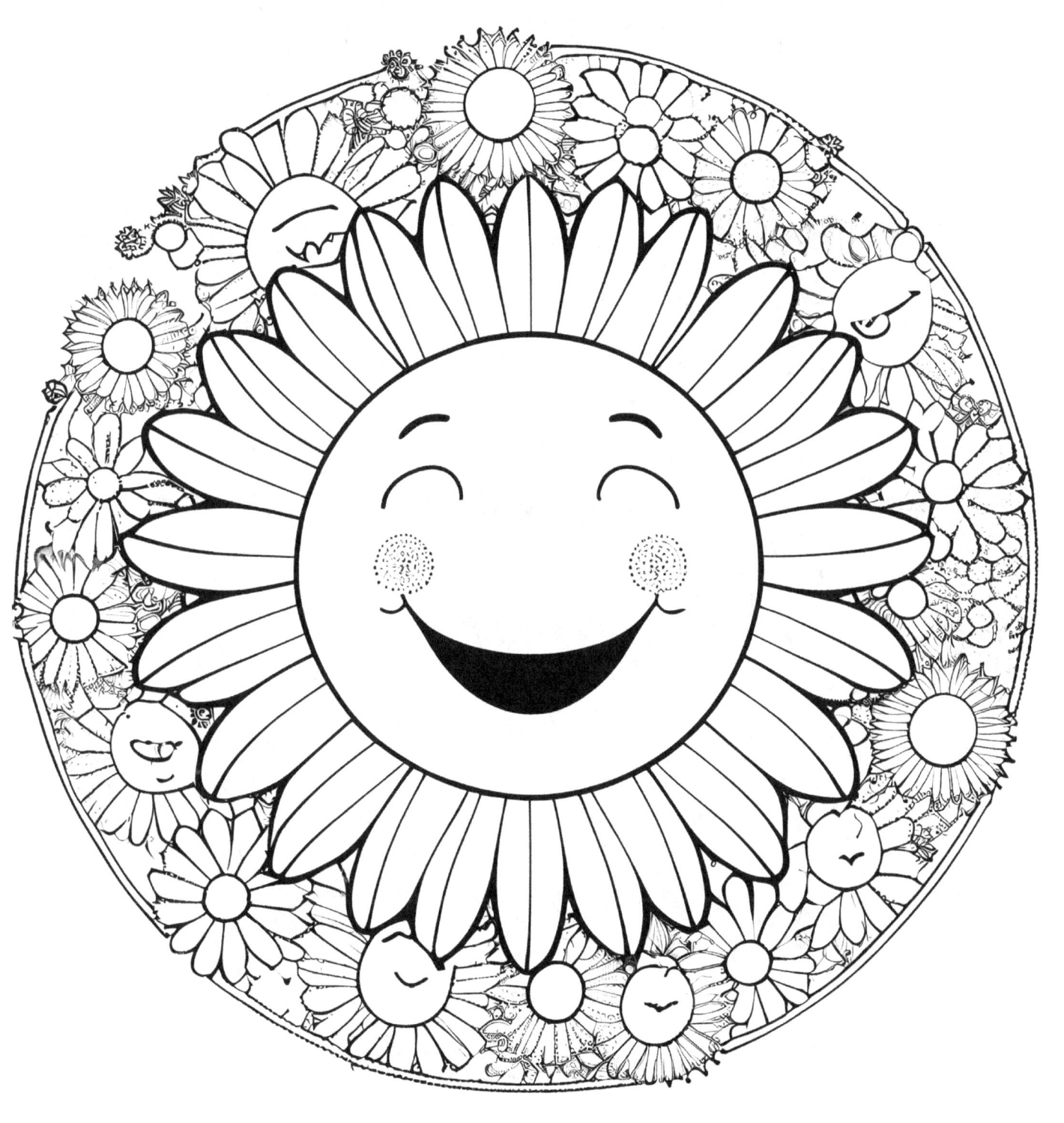

"Life teaches you a new lesson every day, if you are attentive enough in the class of life."

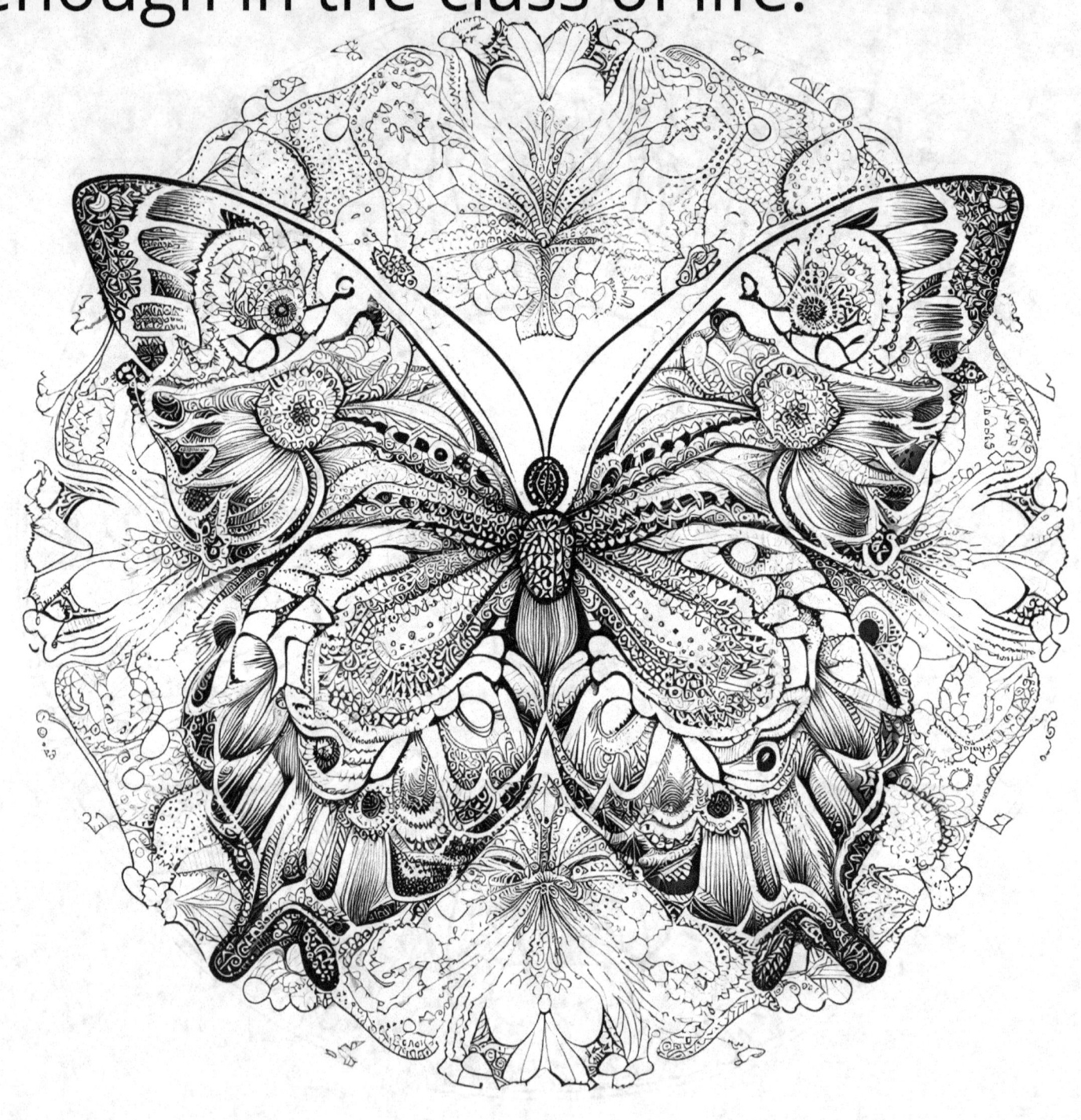

Never let the fear of striking out keep you from playing the game.

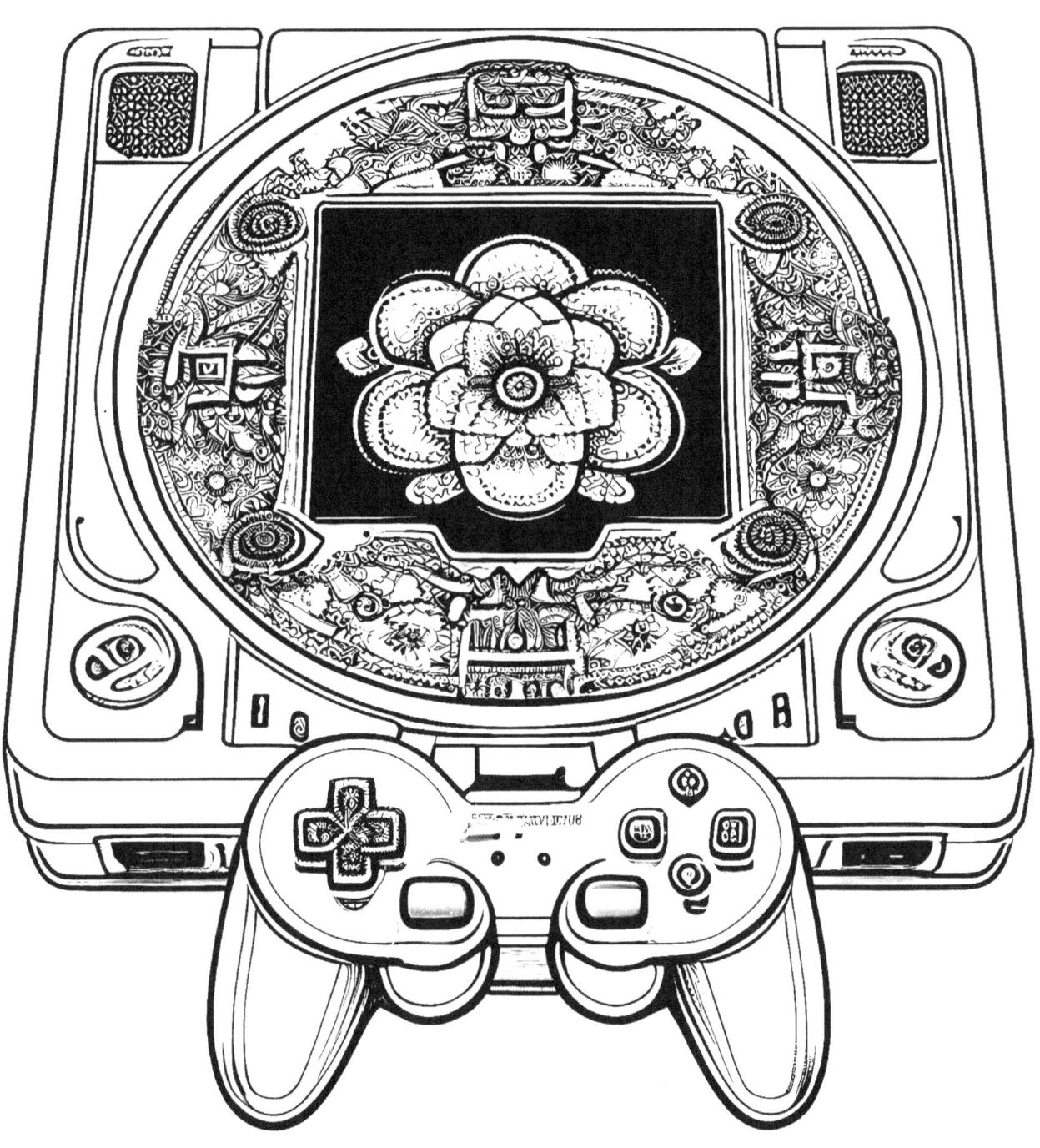

"Remember that not getting what you want is sometimes a wonderful stroke of luck."

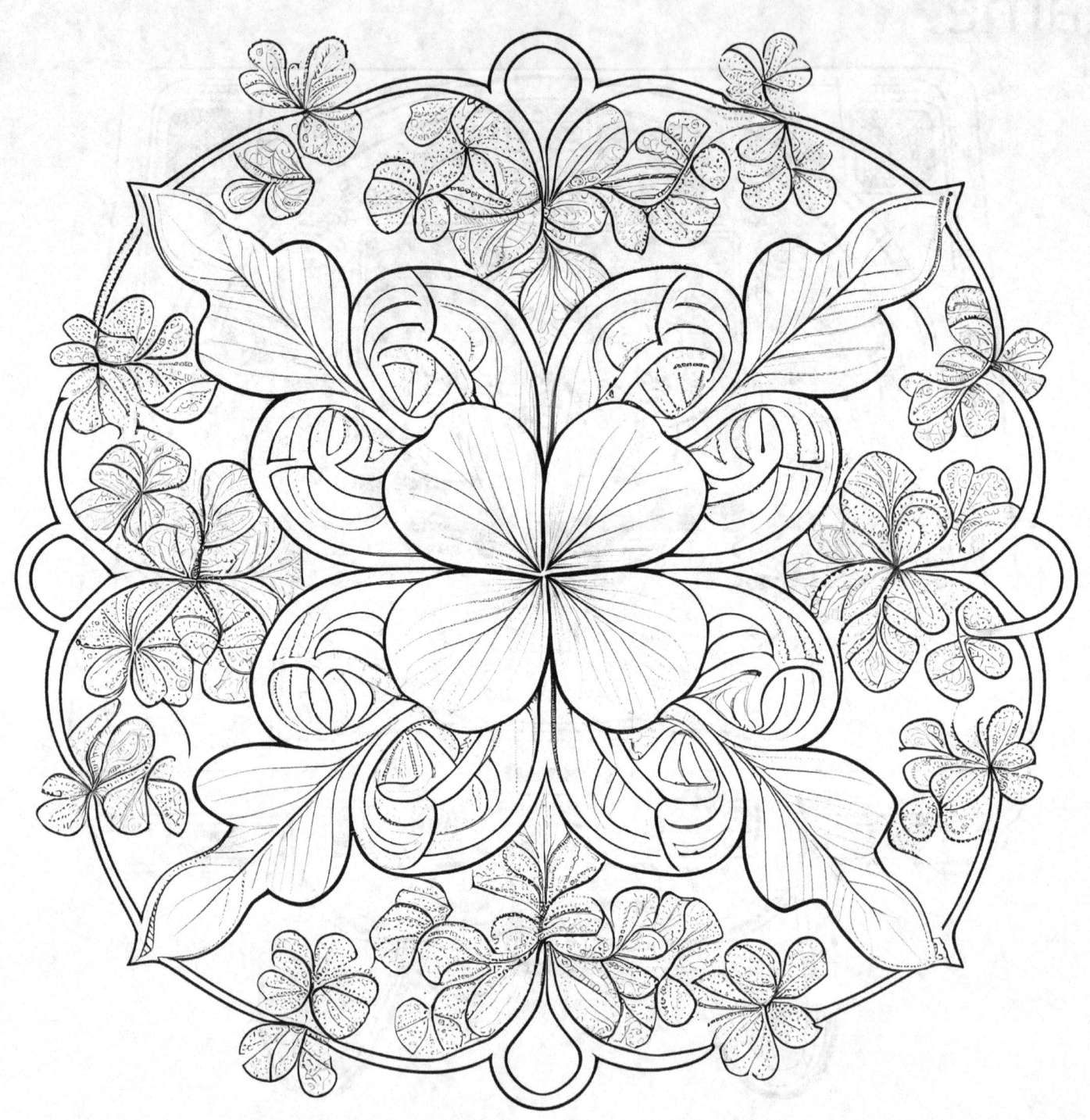

RISE EARLY FIND SOMETHING TO CROW ABOUT!

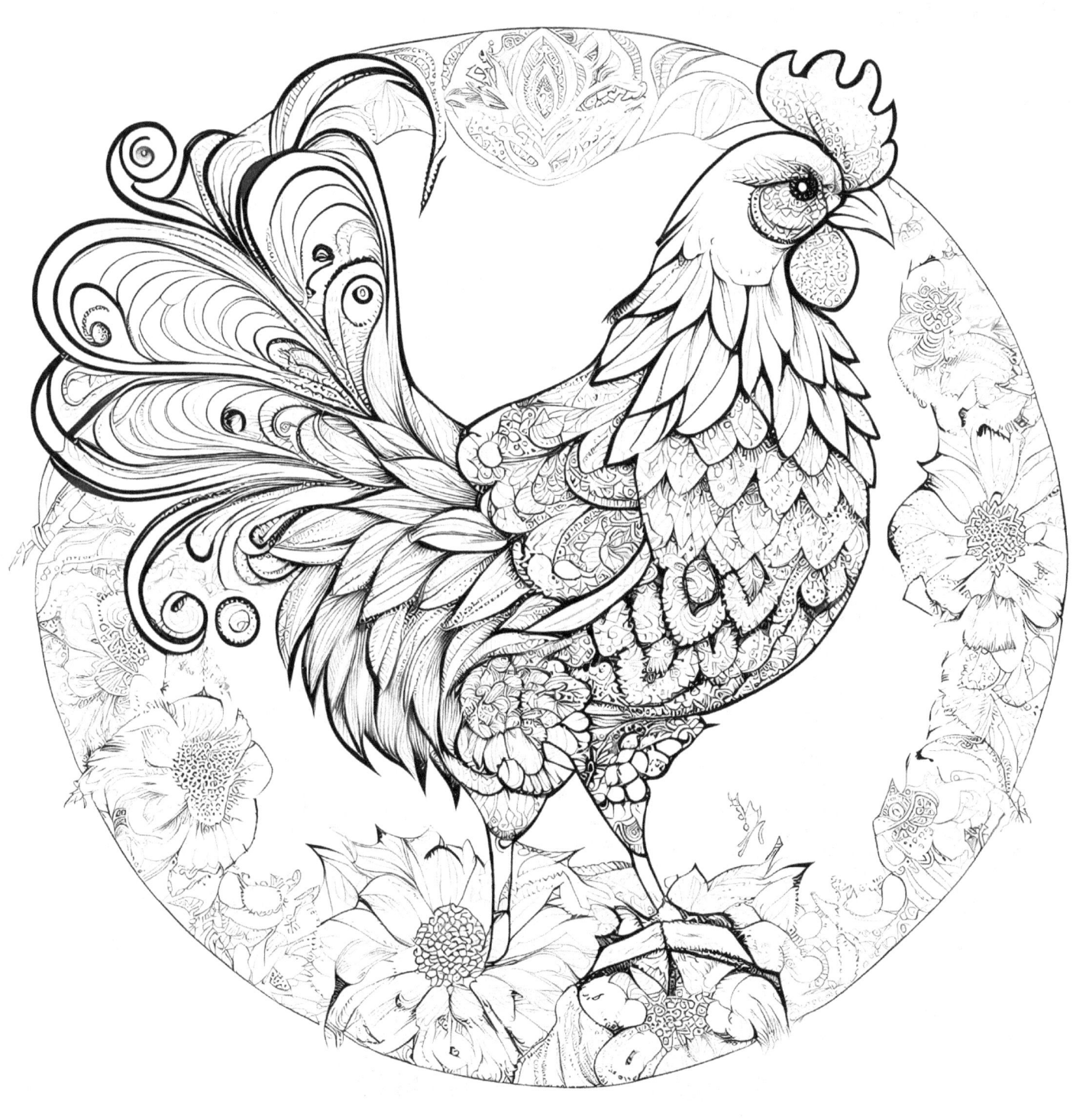

EVERYONE WANTS TO BE A BEAST UNTIL

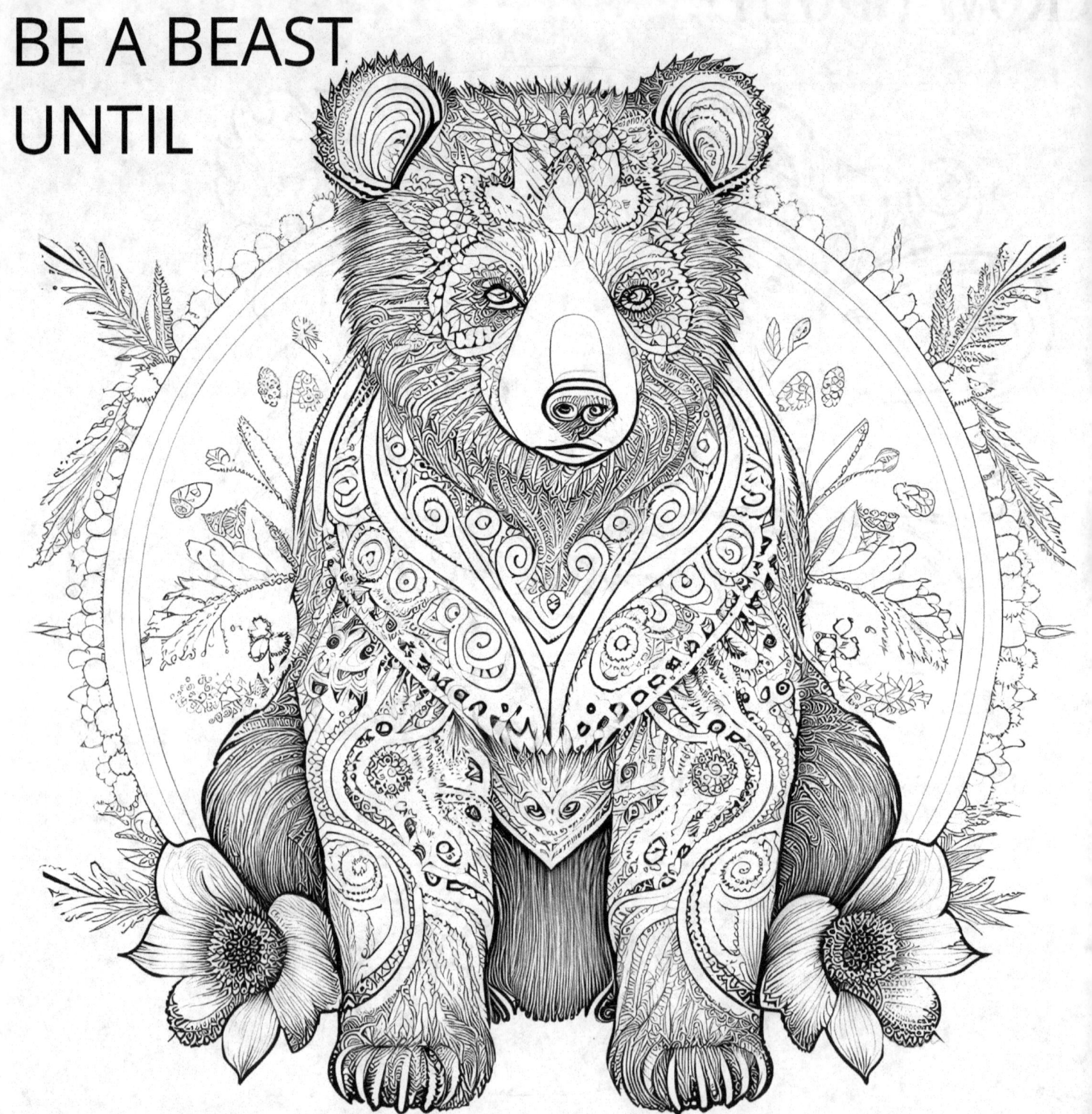

IT'S TIME TO DO WHAT BEASTS DO!